# Most Beautiful Hymns

**ARRANGED BY CAROL KLOSE**

## CONTENTS

Cherry Lane Music Company
Director of Publications/Project Editor: Mark Phillips
Publications Coordinator: Gabrielle Fastman

ISBN 1-57560-854-5

*Visit our website at www.cherrylane.com*

# Abide with Me

Words by
Henry F. Lyte

Music by
William H. Monk

**Moderately slow**

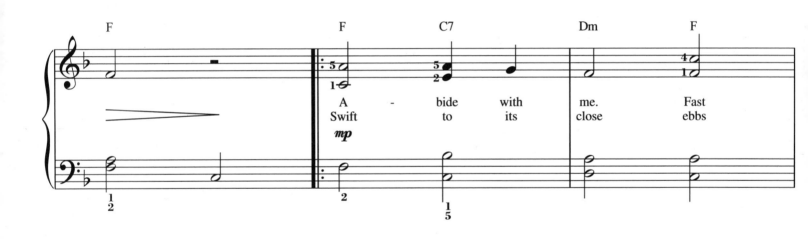

A - bide with me. Fast
Swift to its close ebbs

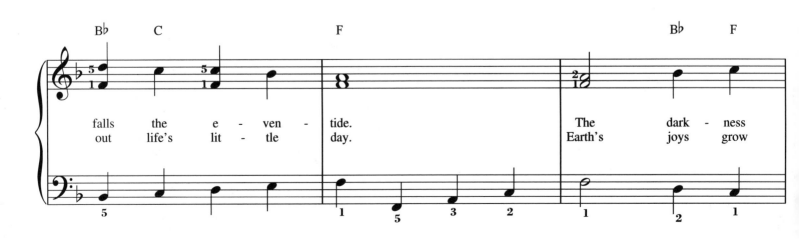

falls the e - ven - tide.
out life's lit - tle day.

The dark - ness
Earth's joys grow

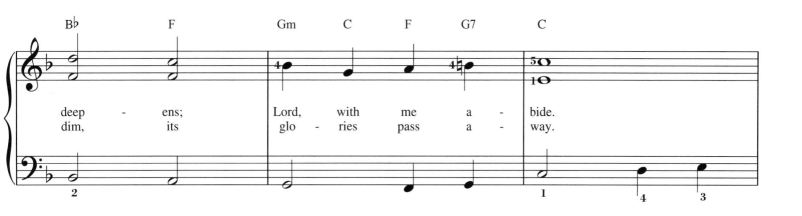

deep - ens; Lord, with me a - bide.
dim, its glo - ries pass a - way.

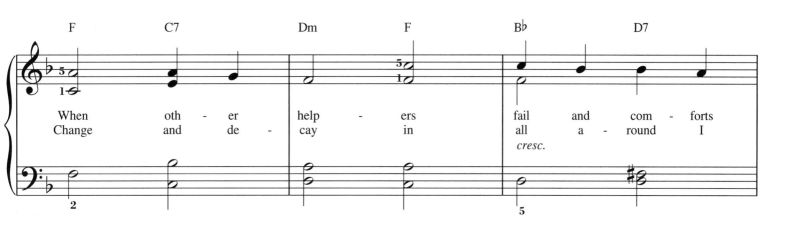

When oth - er help - ers fail and com - forts
Change and de - cay in all a - round I

*cresc.*

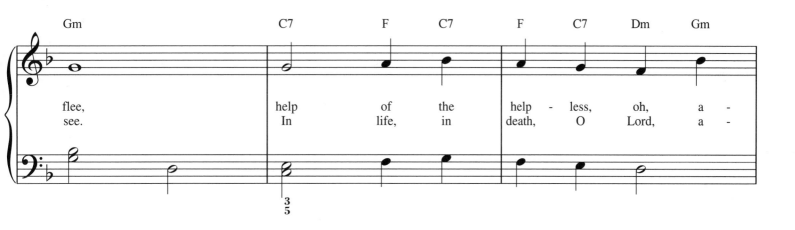

flee, help of the help - less, oh, a -
see. In life, in death, O Lord, a -

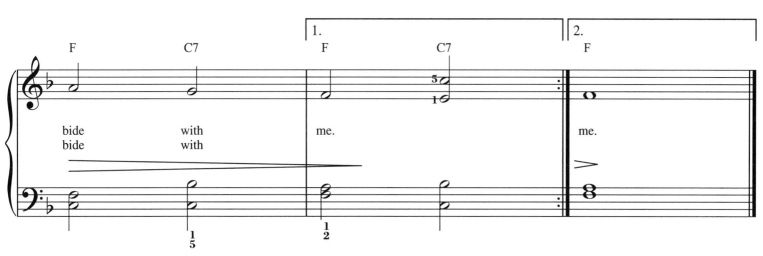

1.

bide with me.
bide with with

2.

me.

# All Creatures of Our God and King

Words by Francis of Assisi
Translated by William Henry Draper

Music from
*Geistliche Kirchengesang*

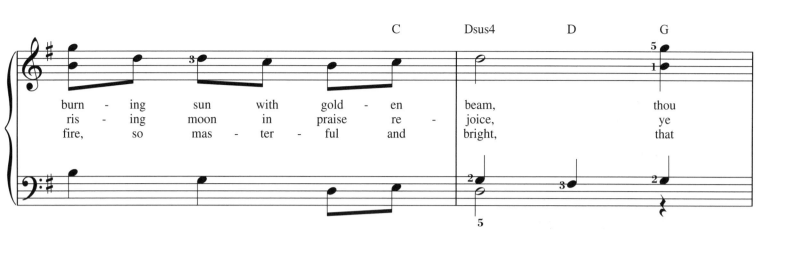

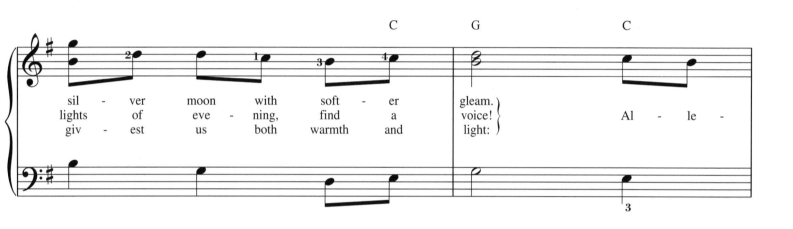

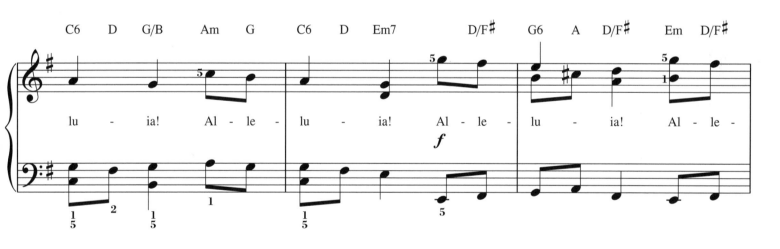

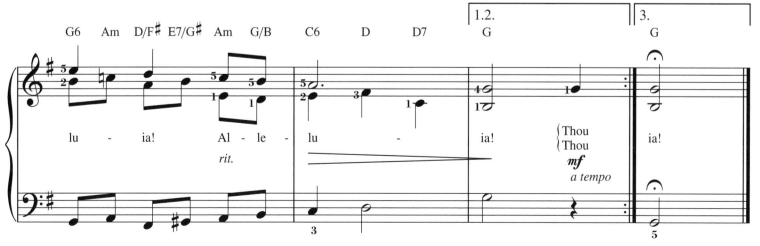

# Amazing Grace

Words by John Newton
From *A Collection of Sacred Ballads*

Traditional American Melody
From *Carrell and Clayton's Virginia Harmony*

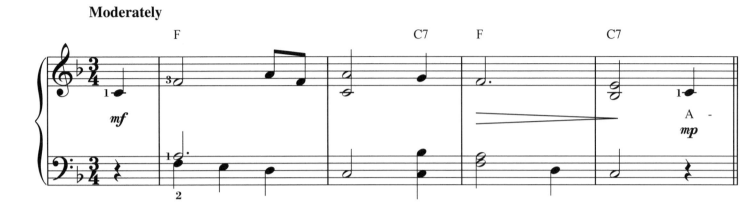

**Moderately**

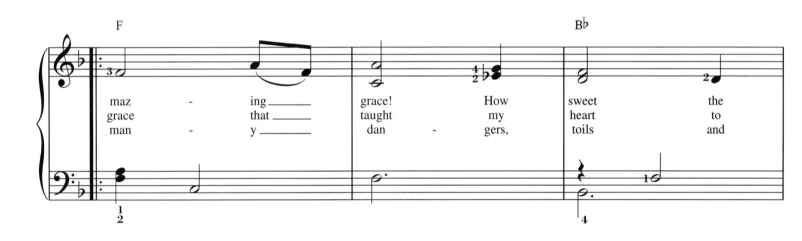

maz - ing _____ grace! How sweet the
grace that _____ taught my heart to
man - y _____ dan - gers, toils and

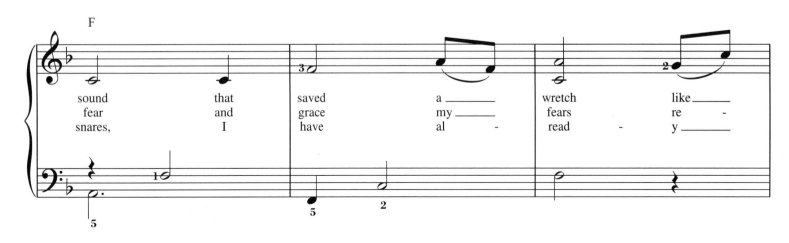

sound that saved a _____ wretch like _____
fear and grace my _____ fears re -
snares, I have al - read - y _____

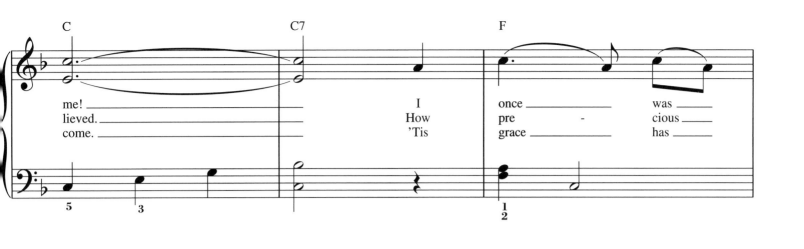

me! _____
lieved. _____
come. _____

I
How
'Tis

once _____
pre -
grace _____

was _____
cious _____
has _____

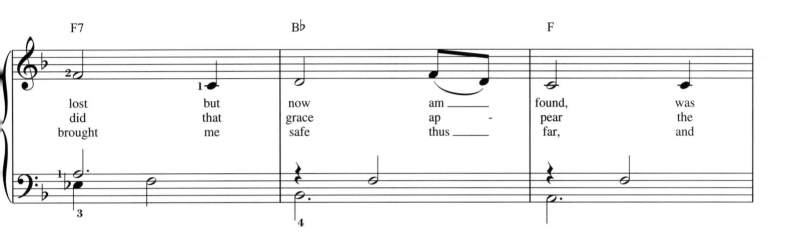

lost
did
brought

but
that
me

now
grace
safe

am _____
ap -
thus _____

found,
pear
far,

was
the
and

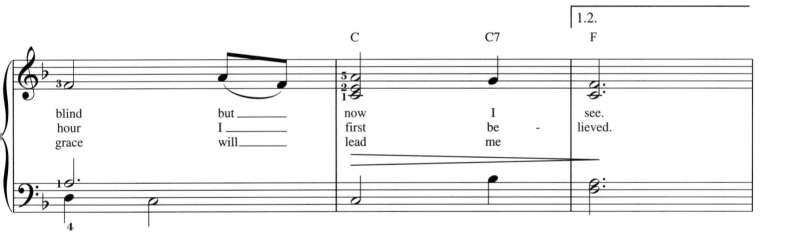

1.2.

blind
hour
grace

but _____
I _____
will _____

now
first
lead

I
be -
me

see.
lieved.

3.

'Twas
Through
*mp*

now. _____

*rit.*

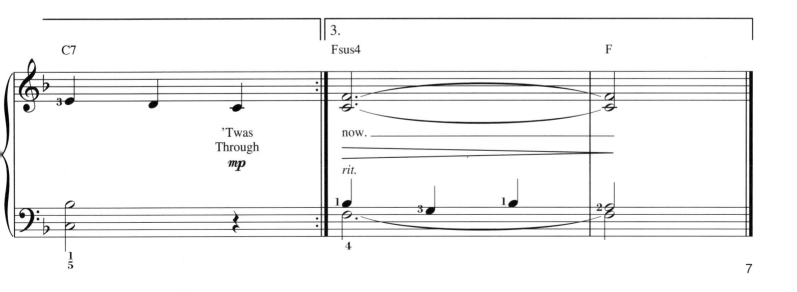

7

# At the Cross

Words by
Isaac Watts and Ralph E. Hudson

Music by
Ralph E. Hudson

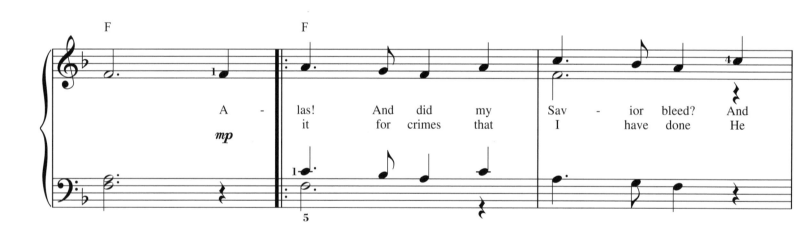

A - las! And did my Sav - ior bleed? And
it for crimes that my I have done He

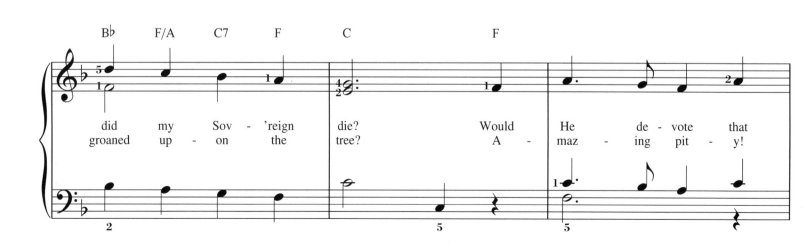

did my Sov - 'reign die? Would He de - vote that
groaned up - on the tree? A - maz - ing pit - y!

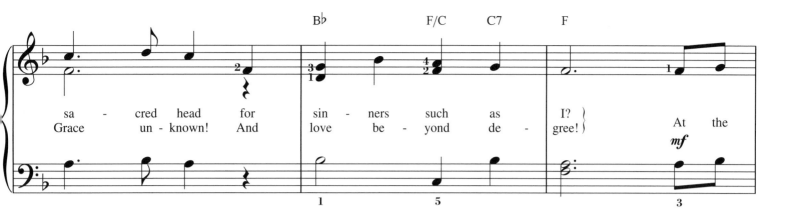

sa - cred head for sin - ners such as I? } At the
Grace un - known! And love be - yond de - gree! } *mf*

cross, at the cross where I first ___ saw the light and the bur - den of my heart rolled a -

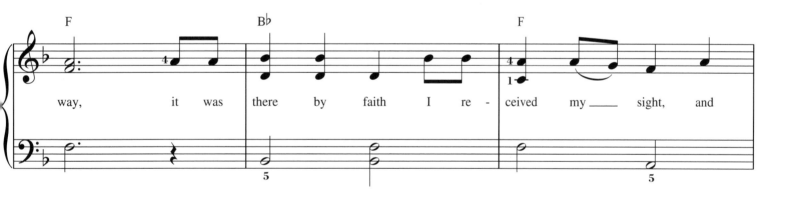

way, it was there by faith I re - ceived my ___ sight, and

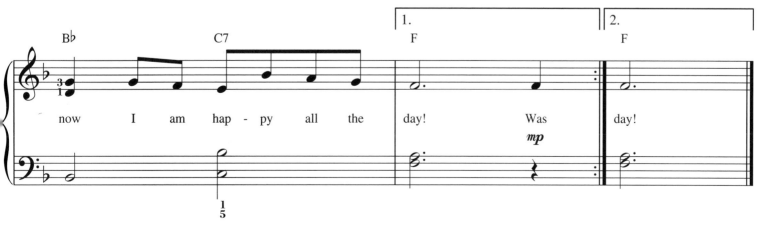

now I am hap - py all the day! Was day!
*mp*

# Battle Hymn of the Republic

Words by
Julia Ward Howe

Music by
William Steffe

**Steady March tempo**

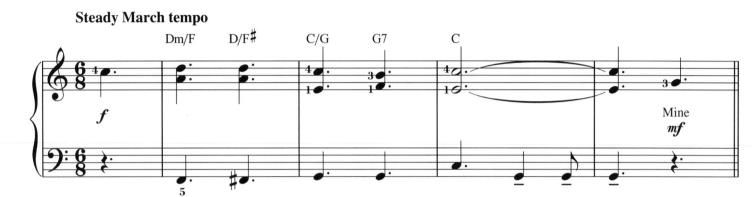

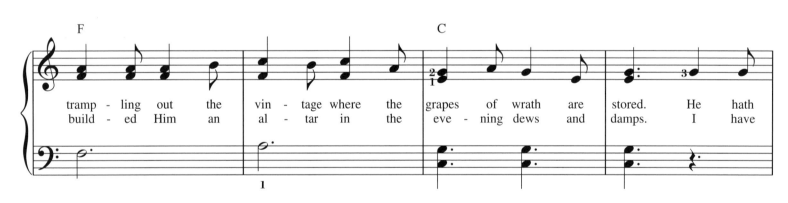

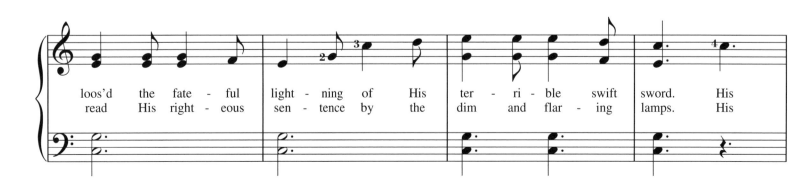

11

# Be Thou My Vision

Translated by
Mary E. Byrne

Traditional Irish

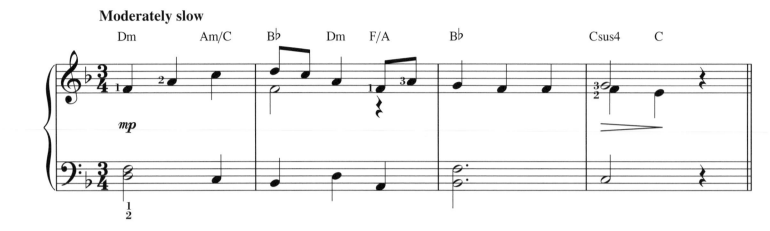

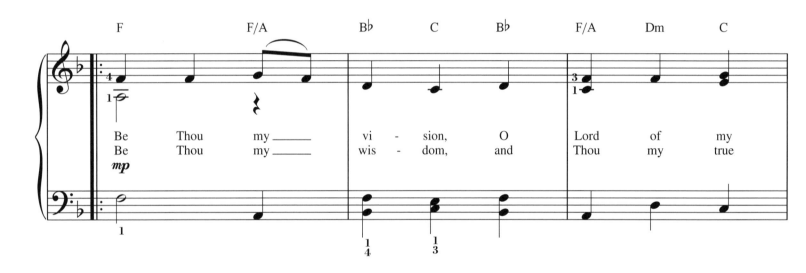

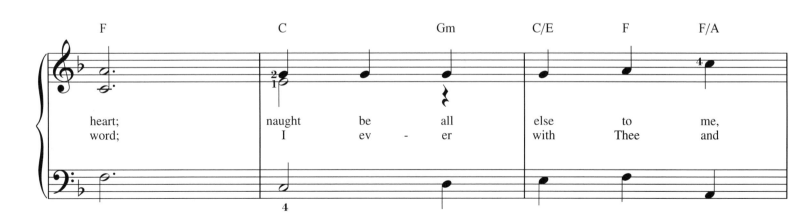

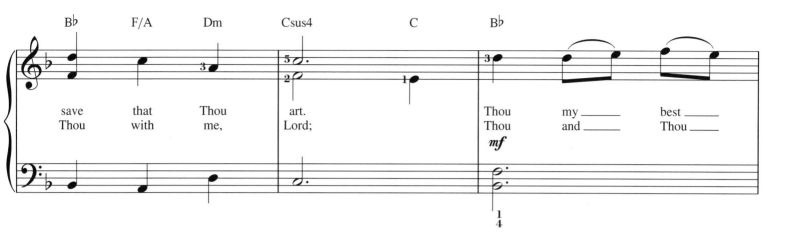

save that Thou
Thou that with me,

art.
Lord;

Thou my best
Thou and Thou

thought by
on - ly,

day or by
first in my

night,
heart,

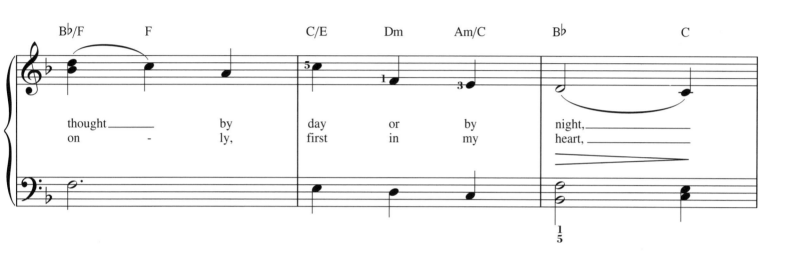

wak - ing or
great God of

sleep - ing, Thy
heav - en, my

pres - ence, my
treas - ure Thou

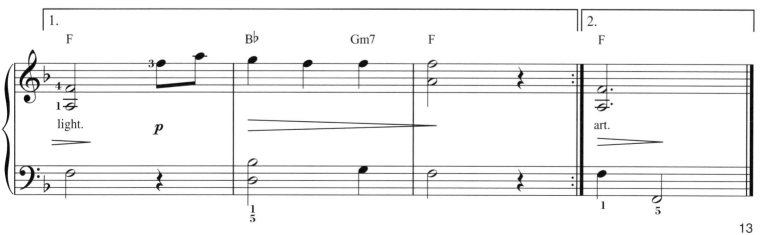

1.

light.

art.

13

# Christ the Lord Is Risen Today

Words by
Charles Wesley

Music adapted from
*Lyra Davidica*

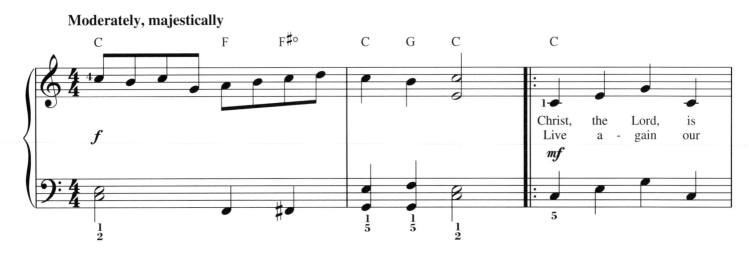

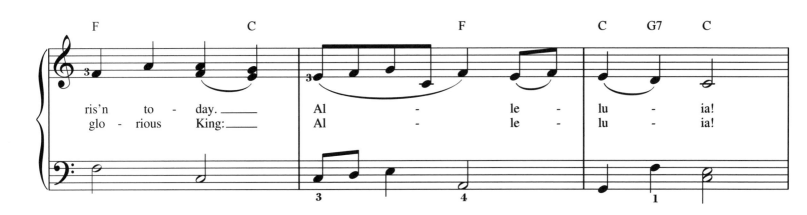

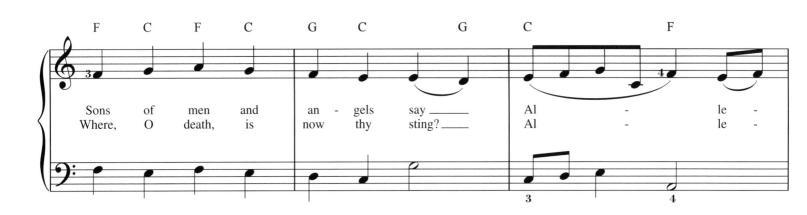

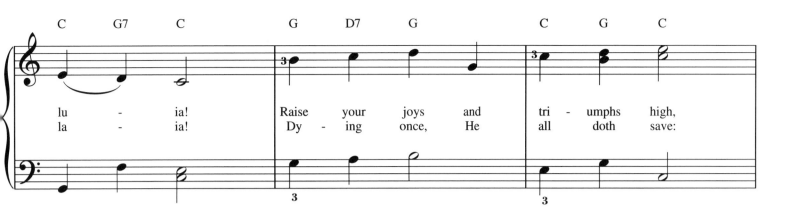

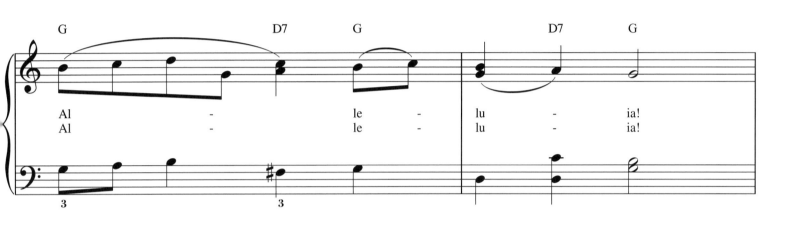

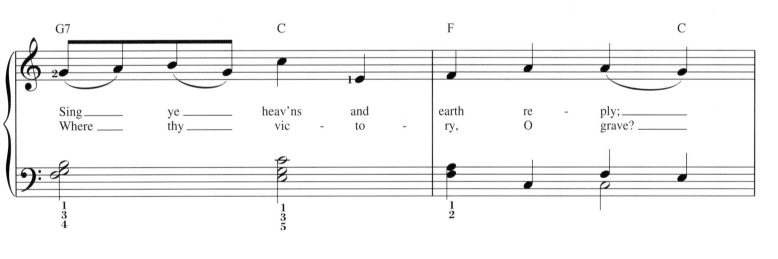

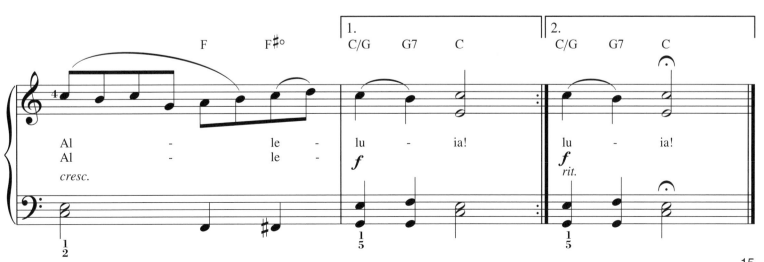

# God of Grace and God of Glory

Words by
Harry Emerson Fosdick

Music by
John Hughes

**Moderately slow**

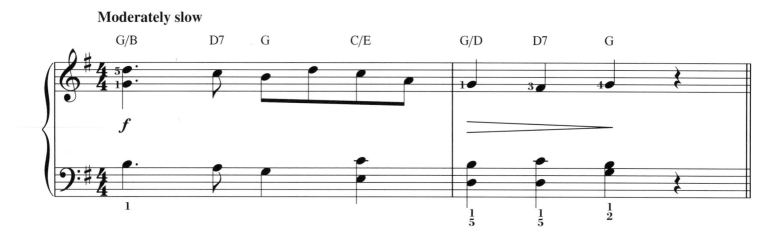

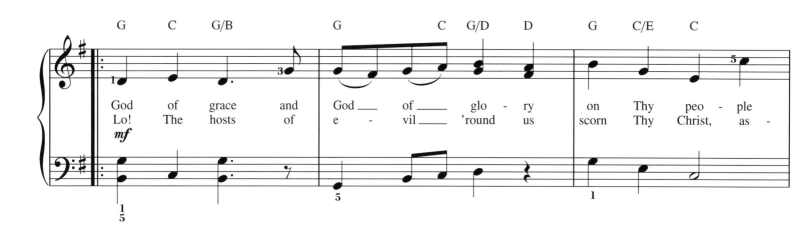

God of grace and God of glory on Thy peo - ple
Lo! The hosts of e - vil 'round us scorn Thy Christ, as -

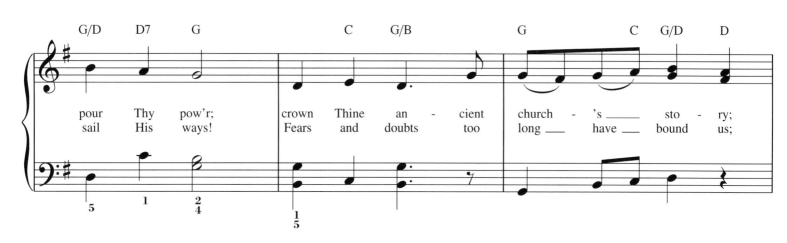

pour Thy pow'r; crown Thine an - cient church's sto - ry;
sail His ways! Fears and doubts too long have bound us;

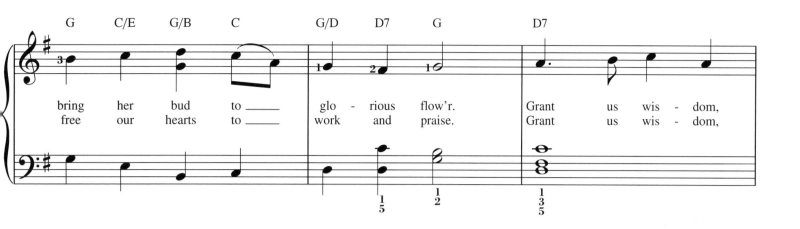

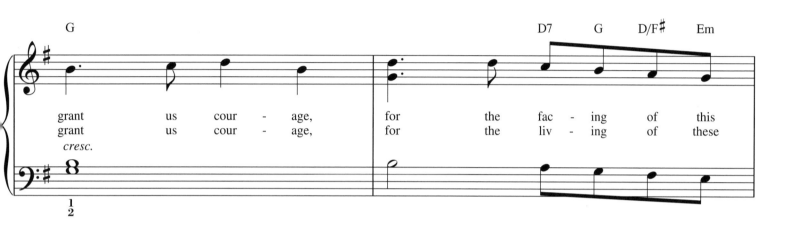

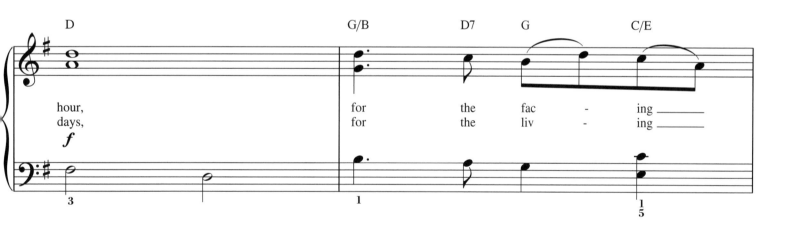

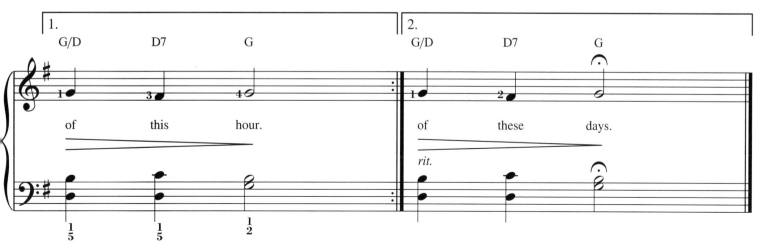

# God of Our Fathers

Words by
Daniel Crane Roberts

Music by
George William Warren

**Moderately, majestically**

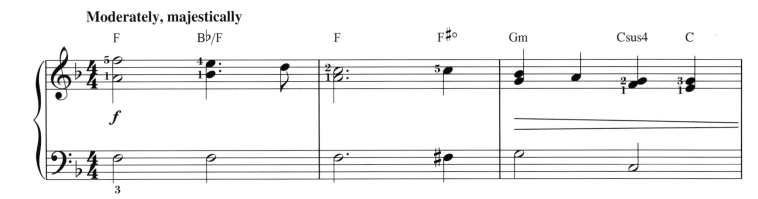

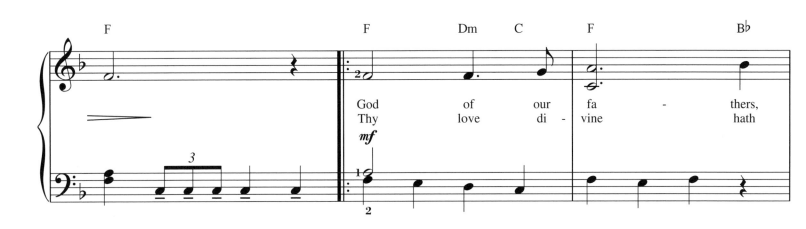

God of our fa - thers,
Thy love di - vine hath

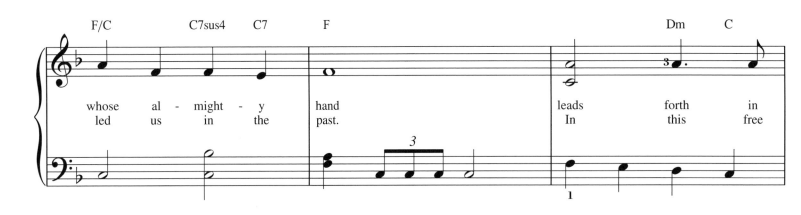

whose al - might - y hand
led us in the past.

leads forth in
In this free

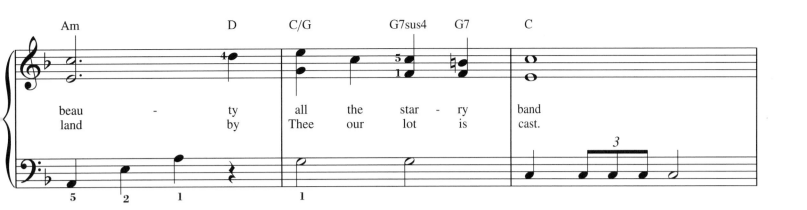

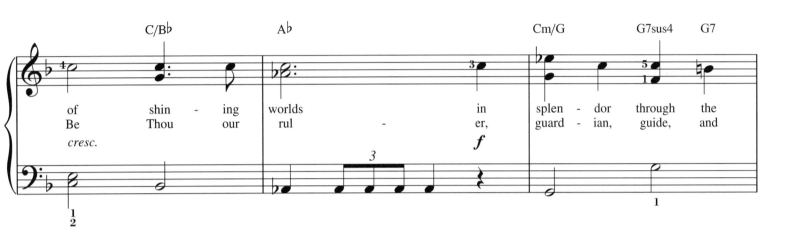

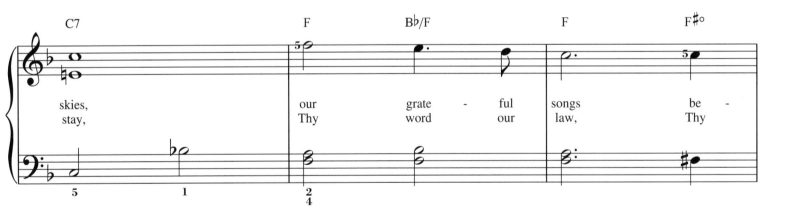

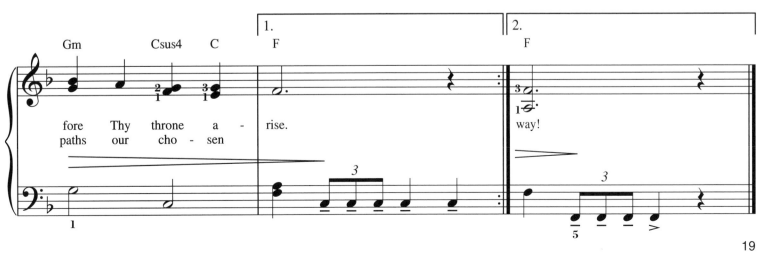

19

# Holy, Holy, Holy! Lord God Almighty

Words by
Reginald Heber

Music by
John B. Dykes

**Moderately, with grandeur**

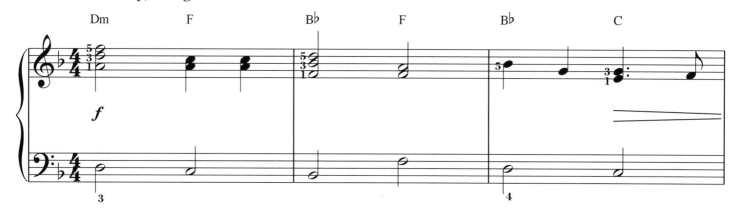

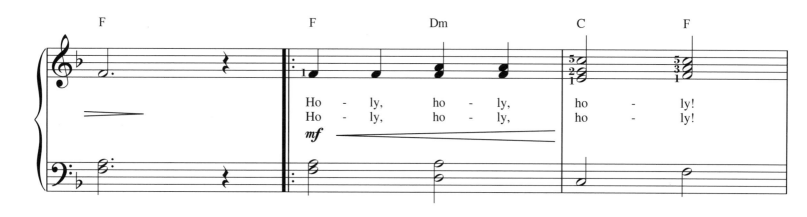

Ho - ly, ho - ly, ho - ly!
Ho - ly, ho - ly, ho - ly!

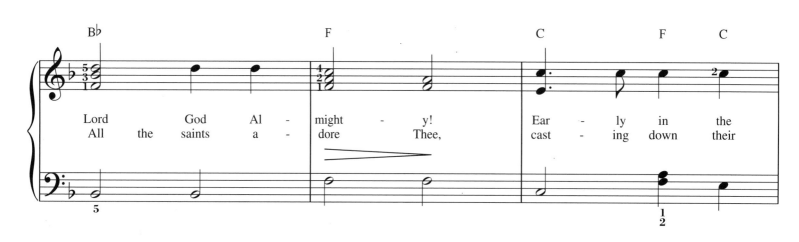

Lord God Al - might - y!
All the saints a - dore Thee,

Ear - ly in the
cast - ing down their

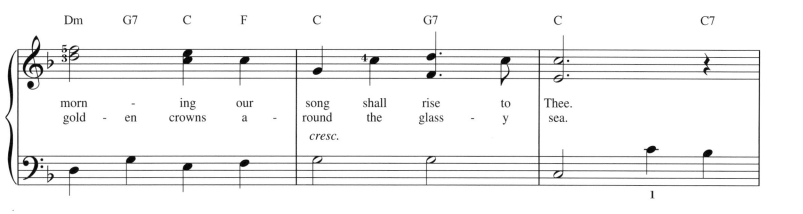

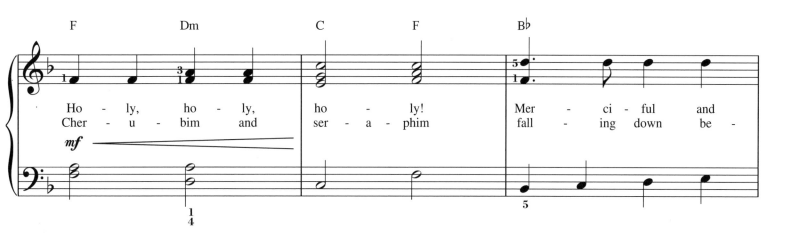

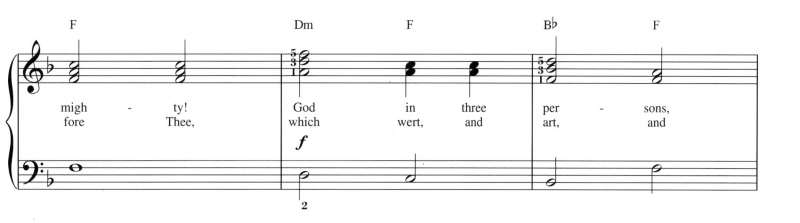

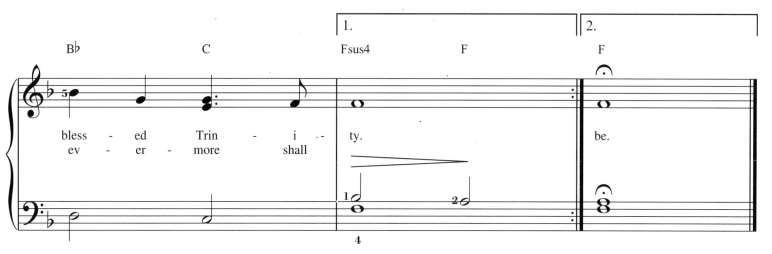

# I Love to Tell the Story

Words by
A. Catherine Hankey

Music by
William G. Fischer

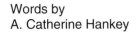

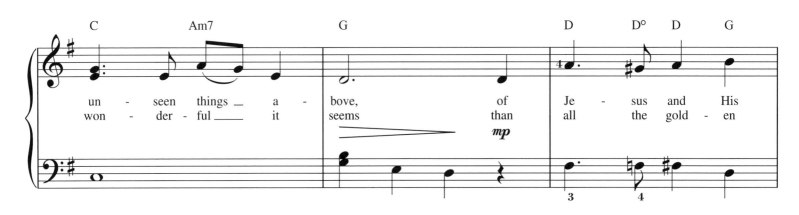

# Just a Closer Walk with Thee

Traditional
Adapted by Kenneth Morris

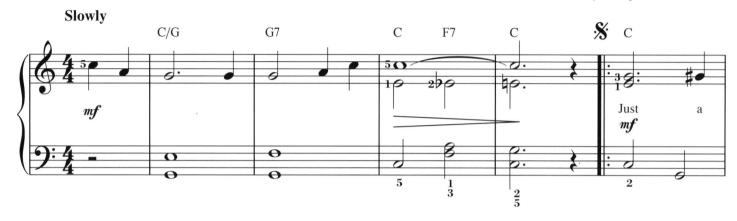

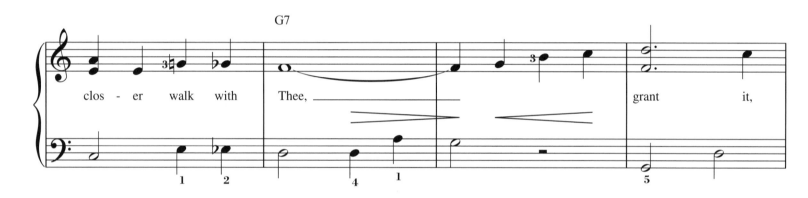

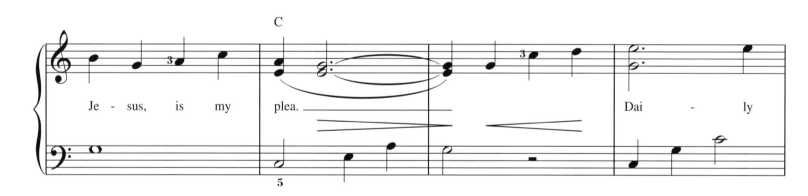

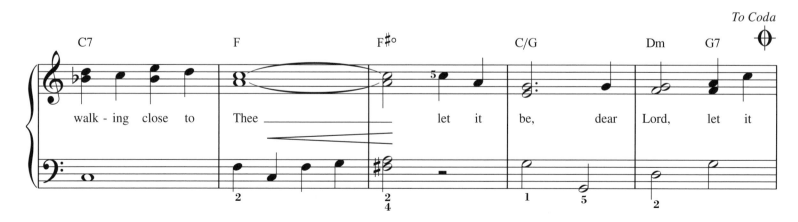

# A Mighty Fortress Is Our God

Words and Music by
Martin Luther

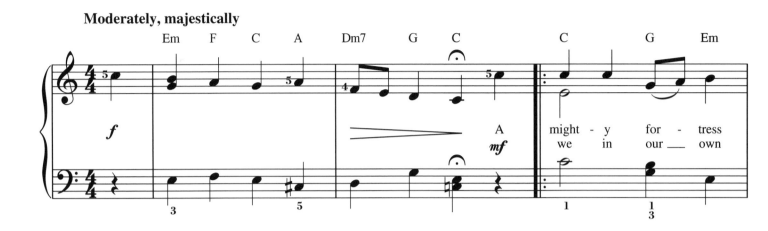

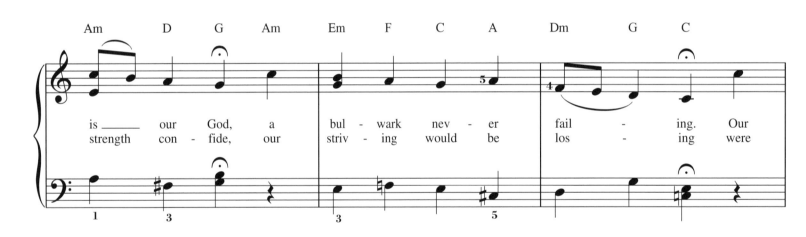

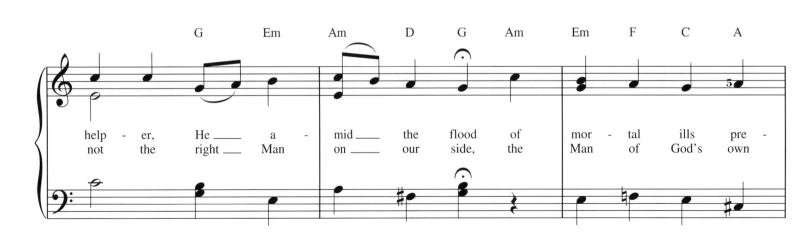

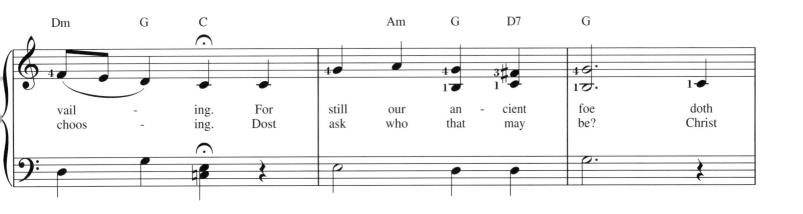

vail - ing. For still our an - cient foe doth
choos - ing. For Dost ask who that may be? Christ

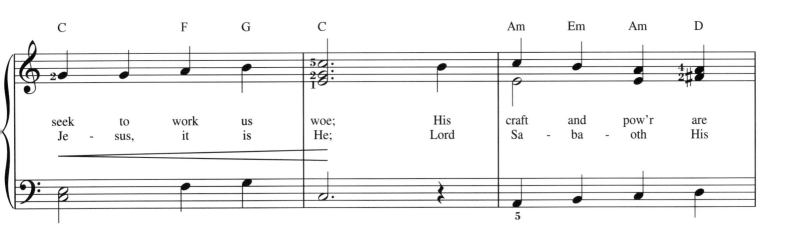

seek to work us woe; His craft and pow'r are
Je - sus, it is He; Lord Sa - ba - oth are His

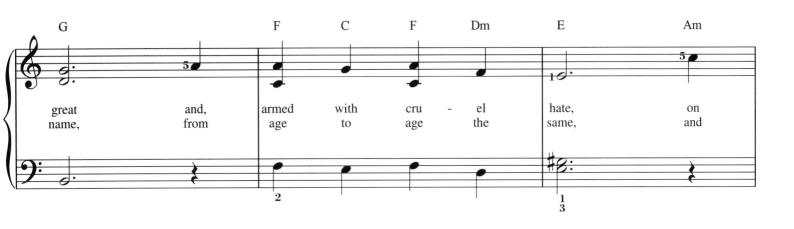

great and, armed with cru - el hate, on
name, from age to age the same, and

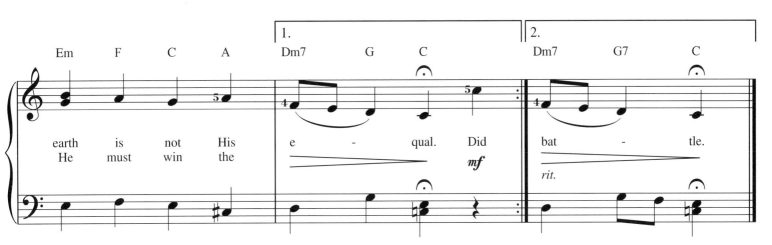

earth is not His e - qual. Did bat - tle.
He must win His

# O Master, Let Me Walk with Thee

Words by
Washington Gladden

Music by
H. Percy Smith

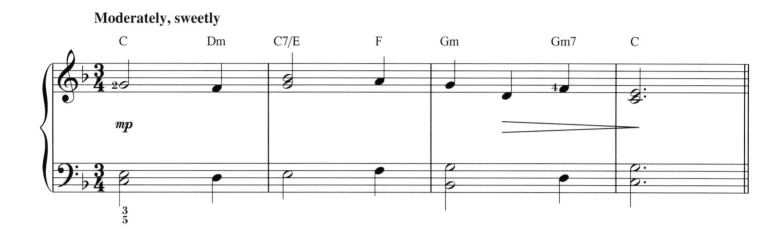

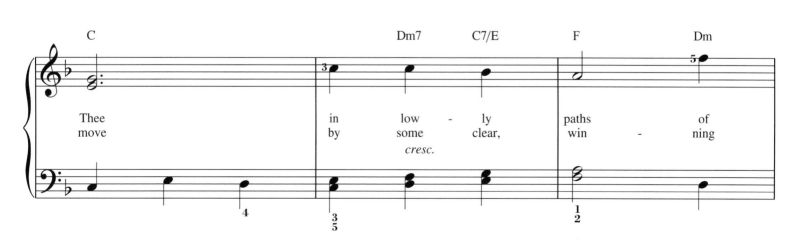

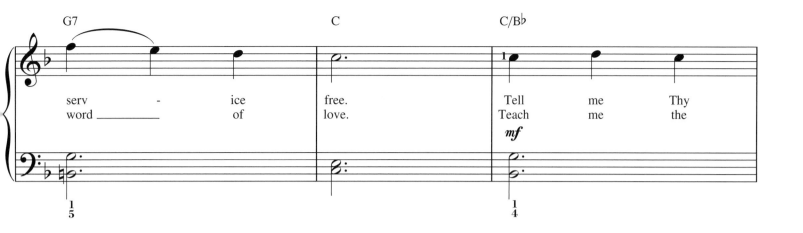

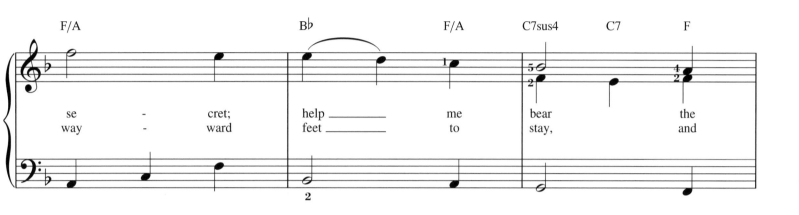

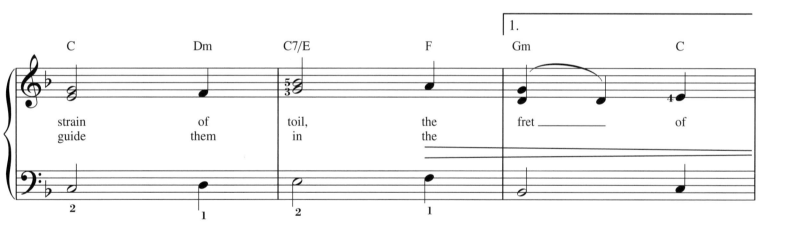

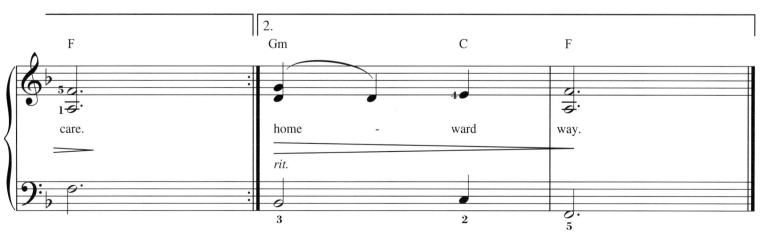

# The Old Rugged Cross

Words and Music by
Rev. George Bennard

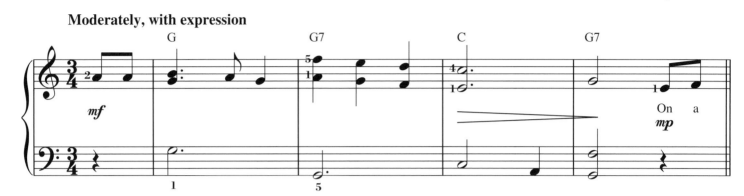

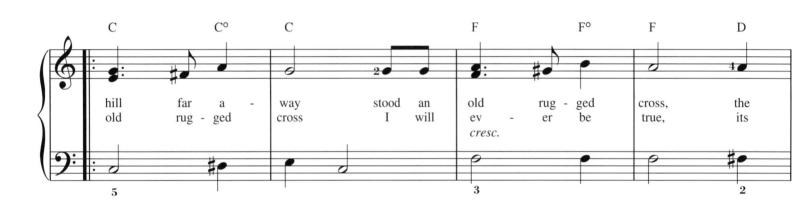

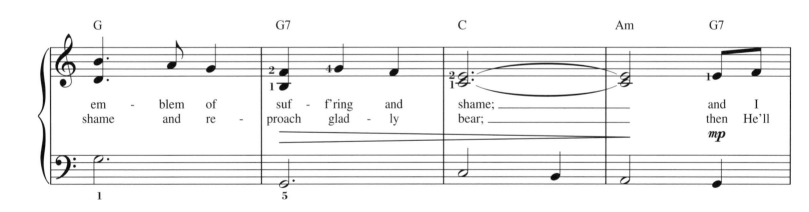

# Onward, Christian Soldiers

Words by
Sabine Baring-Gould

Music by
Arthur S. Sullivan

# Praise to the Lord, the Almighty

Words by Joachim Neander
Translated by Catherine Winkworth

Music from
*Erneuerten Gesangbuch*

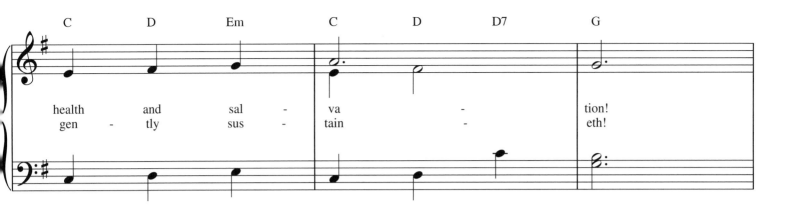

health     and     sal  -  va     -     tion!
gen  -  tly     sus  -  tain     -     eth!

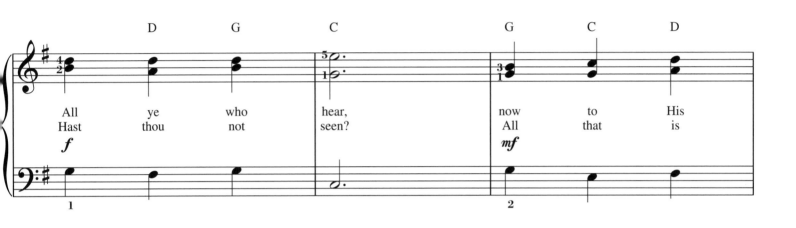

All     ye     who     hear,     now     to     His
Hast     thou     not     seen?     All     that     is

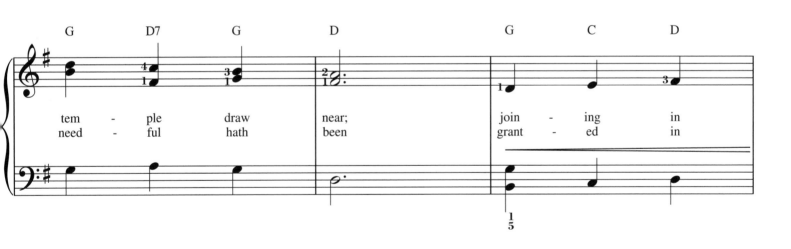

tem  -  ple     draw     near;     join  -  ing     in
need  -  ful     hath     been     grant  -  ed     in

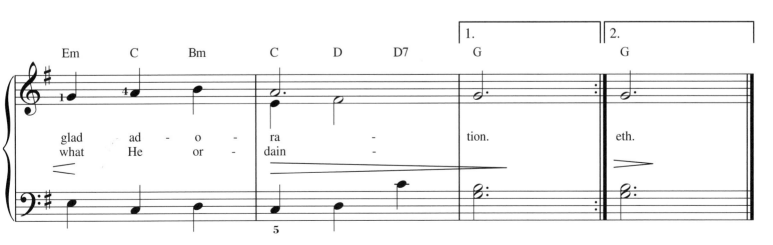

glad     ad  -  o     -     ra     -     tion.
what     He     or  -  dain     -     eth.

35

# Rock of Ages

Words by
Augustus M. Toplady

Music by
Thomas Hastings

**Steady moderate tempo**

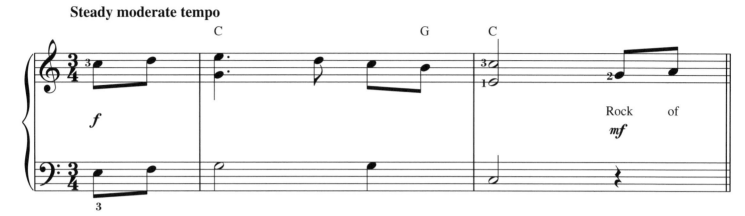

Rock of

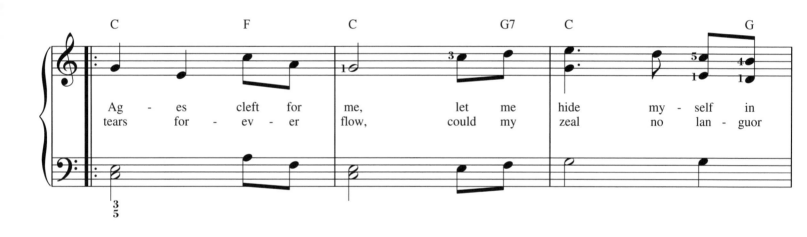

Ag - es cleft for me, let me hide my - self in
tears for - ev - er flow, could my zeal no lan - guor

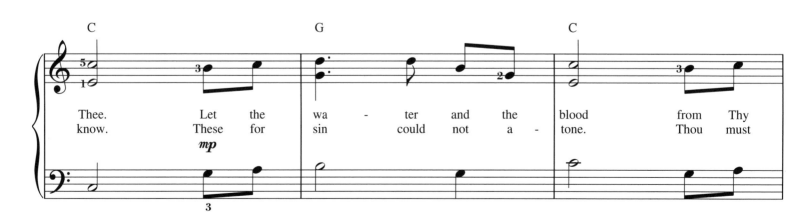

Thee. Let the wa - ter and the blood from Thy
know. These for sin could not a - tone. Thou must

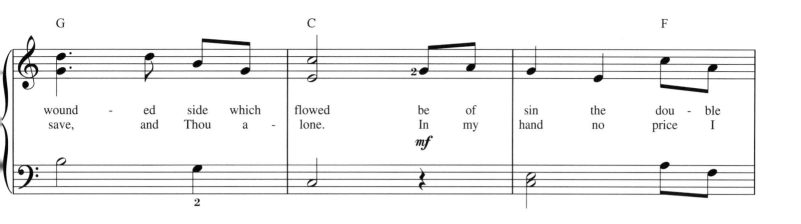

wound - ed side which flowed be of sin the dou - ble
save, and Thou a - lone. In my hand no price I

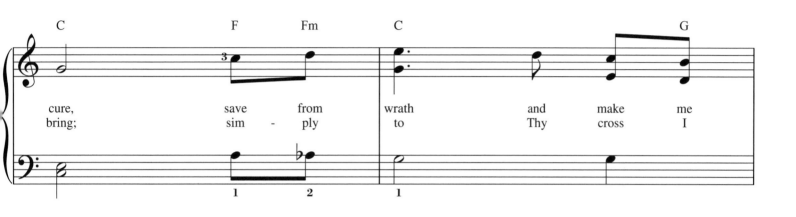

cure, save from wrath and make me
bring; sim - ply to Thy cross I

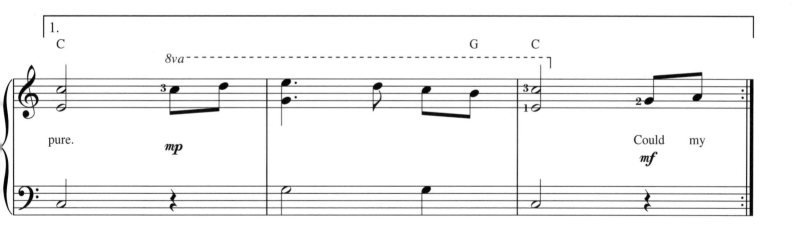

1.

pure. Could my

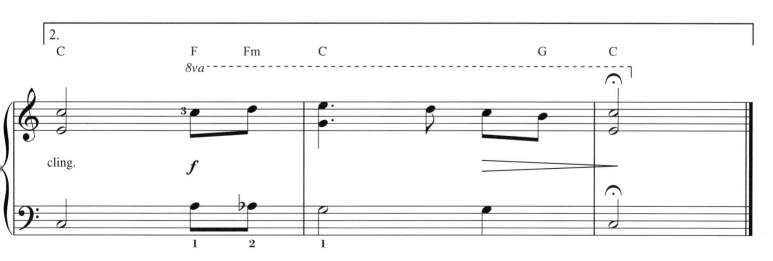

2.

cling.

# Softly and Tenderly

Words and Music by
Will L. Thompson

# We Gather Together

Words from *Nederlandtsch Gedenckclanck*
Translated by Theodore Baker

Netherlands Folk Melody
Adapted by Edward Kremser